THE AMAZING, TRUE STORY OF
PAUL REVERE'S
ALL-NIGHT RIDE
TO WARN AMERICA

THE AMAZING, TRUE STORY OF

PAUL REVERE'S ALL-NIGHT RIDE

TO WARN AMERICA

W. DEAN KLINE

Fountainwood Press

Illustrations by US Illustrations.

First Edition: April 2025

Published by:

Fountainwood Press

1530 Sun City Boulevard

Suite 120114

Georgetown, Texas 78633

Email: publisher@fountainwoodpress.com

For my mom, Carol M. Kline

For always believing there was a book inside waiting to
come out

A Note from the Author About the
15-Minute History Series

I love America.

Two hundred and fifty years ago, the founders created a country dedicated to "Life, Liberty and the pursuit of Happiness."

No kings.

No dictators.

A country where the people would govern themselves. It was a radical idea that had never been tried before. And it worked.

What America and Americans have accomplished since is simply amazing. Defeating the strongest army on Earth and earning independence. Flight. The light bulb. Breaking the sound barrier. Setting foot on the moon. America has made the world a much better place.

History is a fascinating subject because no matter how much you study it, there is always more to learn. Small details tell us important things about the people who helped shape our country and our world.

The 15-Minute History Series is designed to give readers a historically accurate introduction to some of the most important moments in American history, starting with our fight for independence.

As you read about the heroes of the past, I hope it will inspire you to learn more and understand more about the great moments in history that have helped shape our world.

Thank you for joining me on this journey.

Dean Kline
Georgetown, Texas
2025

TABLE OF CONTENTS

If force is to be used at last, it must be a very considerable force, and the country must be subdued.

— General Thomas Gage to Lord Dartmouth, 1775

CHAPTER 1

Growing Tensions

By Spring 1775, tensions between America and Great Britain were high.

It had been just five years since the Boston Massacre. On March 5, 1770, five Americans were killed by British troops during a confrontation outside the Old State House.

It had been just two years since the Boston Tea Party when a group of Americans protesting the Tea Act boarded three British ships in the Boston Harbor and dumped 342 chests of tea – worth more than $3 million today – into the harbor.

A furious King George III responded in 1774 with the Coercive Acts. These acts, which Americans called the Intolerable Acts, closed Boston Harbor, limited town meetings and forced townspeople to house British soldiers in their homes.

With so much anger building up on both sides, Britain's General Thomas Gage, Commander in Chief for North America, was worried about the possibility of war.

By the fall of 1774, the Americans – or colonists – had been storing gunpowder in towns around the area to protect themselves in case of conflict with the British, including a large supply in the town of Somerville, Massachusetts, outside of Boston.

An American informant told General Gage about the supply of gunpowder in Somerville. He decided to act.

Gage picked 250 of his best soldiers and ordered them to travel by boat the seven miles up the Mystic River from Boston to Somerville to capture the gunpowder.

They left early in the morning on September 1st on their mission.

CHAPTER 2

The Powder Alarms

Paul Revere was born in Boston on New Year's Day, 1735, the second of 12 children.

His father, Apollos Rivoire, had traveled from France to start a new life in America, free from religious persecution.

Once he arrived, Apollos began a successful career as a silversmith. He met and married Deborah Hichborn from a wealthy Boston family. He soon changed his last name to Revere and they started a family.

Paul's father had strong feelings about freedom and individual responsibility that helped shape young Paul Revere and led him to a life dedicated to the cause of freedom in America.

By 1774, Paul Revere was a successful silversmith like his father. He was also well known by both his fellow patriots and the British as someone dedicated to the American cause of freedom, frequently riding great distances across rugged roads to alert towns in the area about British plans or important news. His travels took him as far as New York City and Philadelphia.

When he learned about General Gage's plans to capture the gunpowder in Somerville, he rode quickly to warn the town. Unfortunately, he was too late – the British had successfully captured the gunpowder without firing a shot.

The day's events caused panic. False rumors swirled that British soldiers had fired on the colonists, that a large number of warships had arrived in Boston Harbor and that America was under attack.

In response, nearly 4,000 militia – civilians who organized into a local army to protect their communities – hurried from surrounding towns, gathering outside of Boston to help. The turmoil became known as the "Powder Alarms."

The situation was reaching a boiling point.

CHAPTER 3

Discovering the British Plans

After the Powder Alarms, the colonists set up ways to spread the word when the British were on the move. The signals they developed included firing guns in the air, ringing church bells, lighting warning fires and sending riders from town to town.

By early April 1775, the Americans saw signs of a British plot to seize the gunpowder and weapons stored at Concord, a town about 20 miles from Boston.

The British were seen preparing transport boats in the harbor. More troops than usual marched through town. British officers were spotted mapping the roads out of town.

These and other clues led the Americans to guess the British were planning a raid.

And the Americans were right.

General Gage's orders were to march quickly and secretly "to Concord where you will seize and destroy all the Artillery, Ammunition, Provisions, Tents, Small Arms, and all Military stores whatever."

Paul Revere was given the job to warn Lexington, Concord, and other nearby towns that the British were planning to go on the march. He rode from town to town meeting with patriot leaders and exposing the British plans.

His trips included visiting two of the leading patriots who had fled Boston and were staying in Lexington – Samuel Adams and John Hancock.

The Americans were afraid the British were planning to kidnap these two important leaders which would be a devastating blow to the patriot cause.

April 1775 was an anxious time in Boston and the surrounding towns. The British and Americans were both on high alert.

CHAPTER 4

Revere's Assignment

The events on April 18th, 1775, began to unfold quickly.

Paul Revere was at home when a livery boy who worked in the local horse stable came rushing to his house.

"The regulars are on the march!" (Regulars were soldiers in the British Army.)

Meanwhile, Dr. Joseph Warren, one of the most important leaders of the patriot cause, heard from a secret source about British plans to move on Concord. His informant also shared that they were planning to capture Samuel Adams and John Hancock.

He sent an urgent request to Paul Revere to come to his house for instructions. Revere received the message about 9:00 p.m. that evening and hurried to Dr. Warren's house.

Warren instructed Revere that he should go to Lexington to warn Samuel Adams and John Hancock. Warren also told him that fellow patriot William Dawes was riding to Lexington, heading south across the Boston neck and around the outskirts of the city to avoid British patrols.

Revere was to head north and meet up with Dawes in Lexington to help complete their mission of protecting Adams and Hancock.

After getting his instructions, he left Dr. Warren's house about 10:00 p.m.

CHAPTER 5

"Two If By Sea"

Paul Revere had already worked out a plan in case riders were blocked from getting out of town when the British army went on the offensive.

He had discussed his plan with patriots across the water in nearby Charlestown. If they saw one lantern in the steeple of the Old North Church, the British were traveling by land. If there were two lanterns, the British were traveling by sea across the harbor.

In 1775, the Old North Church was the tallest building in Boston. It was an ideal place for a signal. The patriots in

Charlestown – more than a quarter of a mile away – would be alerted to the British movement and could spread the word throughout the countryside.

To complete his plan, Revere asked for help from three friends and fellow patriots – Captain John Pulling, Thomas Bernard and 23-year-old church sexton, Robert Newman.

They agreed to be ready to help when needed. Their assignment would be to place lanterns in the steeple of the Old North Church.

With his instructions from Dr. Warren in hand, Revere went quickly to Robert Newman's house where he met up with Newman, Pulling, and Bernard.

His instructions: hang two lanterns in the church steeple.

CHAPTER 6

A Steep Climb

While Revere hurried home to prepare for his journey to Lexington, the group of three patriots – Newman, Pulling and Bernard – headed to the church on their important mission.

As the church sexton, or caretaker, Newman had keys to the church. Once they arrived, he unlocked the heavy church doors. Newman and Pulling went inside, while Bernard stood guard.

Newman had hidden two small, square metal lanterns in a closet. He took them out and the two men draped the lanterns around their necks. They began climbing the 154 steps to reach the top of the steeple.

Once they reached the top, they lit the candles, then climbed a narrow ladder that led to the highest window in the church steeple.

As instructed, they held the two lanterns out of the northern window toward Charlestown.

Across the river, Charlestown patriots were watching carefully. Suddenly, they saw two faint lights. The signal Revere had promised was only visible for a few moments, but it was long enough.

The Charlestown men acted quickly. One group went to the water's edge to watch for Paul Revere. Others hurried to find him a horse. They sent another rider out into the countryside to spread the word that the British were on the move.

CHAPTER 7

A Dangerous Boat Ride

While the lanterns were being lit and the Charlestown patriots were moving into action, Paul Revere left his house and went to the harborside where he had hidden a small boat.

He had arranged to meet two friends who were experienced boatsmen to help him get across the Charles River. They were Joshua Bentley, a boat builder, and a patriot named Thomas Richardson.

The two men met Revere by his boat hidden under the wharf. The three climbed in, balanced themselves in the small boat, pushed off into the harbor and began rowing toward the Charlestown Ferry landing.

Suddenly, they saw the British warship HMS *Somerset* in their path!

The *Somerset* was a huge, powerful sailing ship with 64 guns and large enough to carry more than 500 sailors. The ship was used to patrol the coast, enforce naval blockades and other important duties.

They sat quietly in the boat as they carefully rowed past the *Somerset*. If caught, their lives would be in danger.

It was a bright night, but the moon was partly hidden at that moment and they were able to safely row past the warship without being detected. Thanks to good fortune and the skill of his friends, Revere arrived safely at the Charlestown Ferry landing.

CHAPTER 8

Onward to Lexington

The Charlestown patriots had planned well.

The group was there to meet Paul Revere as he came ashore, having navigated safely past the HMS *Somerset*.

The group from Charlestown included Colonel Conant of the local militia who escorted Revere from the shoreline to town.

The patriots from Charlestown had arranged for a horse for Revere and warned him to stay alert for British patrols on the road to Lexington.

One of the fastest horses in town belonged to the family of John Larkin, a deacon in the Congregational Church. The horse's name was Brown Beauty, a big, strong, fast saddlehorse. She was surefooted and exactly the type of horse needed for this dangerous journey.

When they arrived at the Larkin barn, Brown Beauty was led out and handed to Paul Revere by Richard Devons, the patriot leader in town.

As Paul Revere described it later, "I set off upon a very good horse... It was then about 11:00 o'clock and very pleasant."

The night was mild and clear, a beautiful spring New England evening.

Paul Revere rode Brown Beauty across Charlestown Neck and turned west toward Lexington. Despite the danger, he was able to appreciate the beautiful spring night.

Suddenly, he saw two horsemen in the distance. As he got closer, he saw military symbols on their hats and pistols poking out from underneath their coats. British regulars!

He spun his horse around in the opposite direction and raced away to escape. They began to chase him. One rider tried to cut him off, but ended up getting stuck in a wet, clay pit.

Paul Revere urged his horse forward. Brown Beauty was fast and surefooted, and they quickly left the other soldier behind.

He kept riding at a gallop all the way to the Mystic River, reaching the small town of Mystic, known today as Medford. He followed the Mystic Road to the village of Monotony, known today as Arlington.

Then he turned west toward Lexington, about a seven-mile ride. He went from town to town spreading the word about the British plans.

With Revere having warned the nearby towns over the last couple of weeks of a possible British plot, other riders were ready and took to their horses to continue spreading the word farther into the countryside.

In each town, militia and Minutemen – militia who were ready at a moment's notice – gathered their muskets and equipment and went on the march to Lexington to meet the British threat.

Meanwhile, back in Boston, the British soldiers were preparing to board the ships that would take them across the harbor and to their march to Concord.

CHAPTER 9

Warning Adams and Hancock

By about midnight, Paul Revere reached the Lexington town square. He passed the Buckman Tavern and traveled a few hundred yards to the home of Lexington's clergyman, Jonas Clark, where he knew Adams and Hancock were staying.

Outside, Sergeant William Munroe stood guard with about a dozen Lexington militiamen.

When Paul Revere came riding up, he called out in a loud voice. Munroe ordered him to quiet down, that people were trying to sleep.

"You'll have noise enough before long! The regulars are coming out!" he replied.

Revere pushed past the militiamen and banged on the door. Reverend Clark stuck his head out of the window, as did a number of his children from their rooms, along with two of the most famous patriots in the country – John Hancock and Samuel Adams.

"Come in, Revere," called Hancock, who recognized him immediately.

Paul Revere entered the home and delivered his message from Dr. Warren to the two patriot leaders.

By now, it was a little past midnight. Revere asked whether William Dawes had arrived yet. He should have been there by then, but there was no sign of him.

To everyone's relief, Dawes arrived a short while later.

They had achieved their mission to warn Hancock and Adams.

Over the next hour or so, they all talked urgently about what to do about the British movements and tried to figure out the exact goals of the British mission.

They decided that there were too many British soldiers headed in their direction for a mission just to capture Hancock and Adams. The British army's main target must be the military stores in Concord.

Concord must be warned. It was up to Revere and Dawes to make the journey.

CHAPTER 10

The Regulars on the March!

Back in Boston, about the time Revere and Dawes were leaving the city, Gage had his army in motion.

He ordered 21 companies of soldiers, about 800 to 900 soldiers, to get on the move.

They had their muskets and full cartridge boxes carrying 36 rounds of gunpowder and musket balls each, along with a day's supply of food and water.

The companies included the Royal Welch Fusiliers, the famous "King's Own" foot soldiers, and many others.

Their orders were to gather by group down at the harbor where the Royal Navy would transport them by large rowboat across to the mainland at the town of Cambridge.

The soldiers lined up and began boarding the boats for the journey. The boarding took longer than expected but they got underway and finally made it across the harbor.

Unfortunately for the British soldiers, they landed in wet marshland. They were forced to march through water, sometimes up to their waist. By the time they reached solid land, many of them were soaked and shivering from cold.

It took more time than expected to get organized for the mission. But soon they were on the march through Cambridge and headed for Lexington and Concord.

CHAPTER 11

Captured!

About the time the British soldiers were marching out of Cambridge, Paul Revere and William Dawes were leaving Lexington together on their next mission: to alert Concord.

They hadn't been riding long when they met up with a doctor from Concord, Dr. Samuel Prescott. They began to ride together and it was clear that Dr. Prescott was a strong supporter of the patriot cause. He offered to help spread the word about the British plans.

As they rode toward Concord, the three riders worked together to alert as many homes as possible.

About two miles past Lexington, they entered the town of Lincoln. Suddenly, riders came out from the shadows. A British patrol!

Paul Revere called a warning to his two friends but they were quickly surrounded.

One of the British soldiers called out to Revere, "If you go an inch farther you are a dead man!"

As they were led into an open field, they saw an opportunity to make a break for it.

Dr. Prescott, who knew the countryside well, turned his horse to his left, jumped a low stone wall and disappeared into the darkness.

He would be the only one of the three patriot riders to reach Concord and deliver the news about the British army heading their way.

Meanwhile, Paul Revere turned his horse to the right hoping to escape into the woods. As he rode away, six more soldiers on horseback suddenly appeared, surrounding him. He was captured.

In all the confusion, William Dawes was able to get away, riding to the safety of a nearby farm.

As Dawes got close to the farmhouse, his horse got spooked and he was thrown off. Fortunately, he was able to avoid being captured by the nearby British patrol.

He had had enough.

He remounted his horse and began a slow ride back to Lexington, staying in the shadows to keep out of sight.

William Dawes' journey was ended.

CHAPTER 12

Escaped!

While Dr. Prescott was galloping toward Concord, and William Dawes was slowly riding back to Lexington, Paul Revere was being held captive by the British officers.

They began to question him, but he quickly turned the tables. He let them know that he knew their plans to invade the area, that the soldiers had come across the harbor in row boats, and that their mission was to get to Concord.

His confidence surprised the British officers. He told them that the entire countryside was alerted to their plans, that he expected to have 500 men there soon, and *their* lives were in danger, not his.

The more he talked, the more nervous the British officers became. They realized they no longer had the element of surprise. The column of British soldiers on the march could be walking into a trap and needed to be warned.

They began leading Paul Revere and other prisoners they had captured back toward Lexington.

It was about 3:00 a.m. as they approached the town when they heard alarm guns being fired into the air and church bells ringing.

The British officers began to panic. They decided to turn their prisoners loose so they could rush ahead to alert the British column that was on the march.

One of the larger soldiers took Revere's horse, Brown Beauty, and they all galloped away, leaving a tired Revere to walk back to town.

It was the last time he saw Brown Beauty, the courageous horse that had taken him on his historic journey.

CHAPTER 13

Rescuing John Hancock and Samuel Adams

The alarms that Paul Revere and the other riders had spread that night worked. Militia from neighboring towns began marching toward Lexington and soon patriots from all across the area with their muskets in hand were on their way to help.

Meanwhile, a tired Paul Revere reached Lexington. He headed back to the home of Jonas Clark to make sure that Samuel Adams and John Hancock had taken his advice and escaped before the British army's arrival, which was expected at any minute.

He walked in the door and was shocked to see that they were both right where he left them three hours before!

The patriot leaders were debating whether to stand and fight or to escape.

They were finally convinced to depart before the British army arrived. They climbed into John Hancock's carriage and headed out.

Paul Revere escorted them far enough out of town to make sure that they were safely on their way, then returned to Lexington Green.

Having secured the safety of two patriots vital to the cause of freedom, one last assignment was waiting for him when he returned to town.

John Hancock kept a large, heavy wooden trunk filled with secret papers that were vital to the patriot cause. If the British were to find the papers, many lives would be in danger. They needed to be kept out of British hands.

The trunk was located on the second floor of the Buckman Tavern. Hancock's clerk, John Lowell, wanted to move the trunk to a safe place. He needed Revere's help.

Knowing the British had to be close, the two men hurried to the tavern. As they got to the second floor, they saw the trunk in the room where John Hancock had left it.

At that moment, Revere looked out the window and saw British troops approaching up the Lexington Road.

They didn't have much time.

They decided to hide the heavy trunk in some woods nearby.

They struggled moving the heavy trunk down the stairs. They carried it out the front door and directly through the group of militia now gathering on the Lexington Green to greet the oncoming British army and out toward nearby woods.

After a long night of marching, the British column of soldiers finally arrived and came face to face with the patriot militia led by Captain John Parker.

The Americans stood bravely as the British officer in charge, Major John Pitcairn of the Royal Marines, ordered them to lay down their weapons and step aside.

Seeing they were vastly outnumbered, and not wanting to create unnecessary bloodshed, Captain Parker ordered his men to step out of the way of the British.

At that moment, Paul Revere and John Lowell were carrying the trunk safely into the woods. Revere looked over his shoulder to see the confrontation.

Suddenly a shot rang out. He didn't know where it came from, but Revere saw a puff of white smoke in front of the British troops followed by a roar of musket fire.

The American Revolution had begun.

CHAPTER 14

The Aftermath

The Battles of Lexington and Concord on April 19, 1775, began the Revolutionary War.

The next year, Paul Revere officially joined the army with a rank of lieutenant colonel. He was assigned to protect Boston against a potential British attack.

The war would last until 1783 when America won her independence from Britain and a new nation was born, a country founded on liberty, that would be governed by the people, not dictators or kings.

After the war, Revere returned to his work as a silversmith, becoming one of the most famous artisans of the era.

Because of his courage and commitment to the cause of freedom, Paul Revere deserves to be remembered as one of our earliest American heroes, along with the other riders who bravely traveled throughout the countryside to warn their fellow patriots about the British march on Lexington and Concord on April 18th and 19th, 1775.

CHAPTER 15

The Rest of the Story

There are many stories to tell about Paul Revere and his all-night ride. Here are some fascinating facts that help tell more of the story of that important moment in history.

The Old North Church

Today, the Old North Church is a beautiful building with its white steeple stretching high into the sky in North Boston.

At the time, it was known as a church for loyalists, people who were loyal to the king rather than the patriot cause, so it's ironic that it would play such an important role in helping alert the patriots about the British plans.

Located just around the corner from Paul Revere's home, the Old North Church is open to the public where you can visit, tour the grounds and the church, and see the steeple where the two famous lanterns were hung.

Robert Newman and Captain John Pulling

Following the Battles of Lexington and Concord, church sexton Robert Newman and Captain John Pulling were both suspected of conspiring to help warn the patriots about the British plans.

Robert Newman was arrested by the British but was later released because of a lack of evidence.

Captain Pulling was hunted by the British army. Local folklore tells a story of how he hid in a wine cask in his mother's house to avoid being captured. He later fled Boston disguised as a sailor.

Their actions that night remain an important part of American history.

The HMS Somerset

The HMS *Somerset*, the massive warship that blocked Paul Revere's way during their ride across the harbor, had a surprising fate.

In November 1778, three years into the war, the *Somerset* was sailing from New York to Boston Harbor when it was hit by a deadly storm. The wind and waves washed over her decks and the sails were ripped apart.

The ship ran aground near the town of Truro on Cape Cod. In the midst of the wild storm, the crew cut down the masts and threw cannons overboard, hoping to lighten the ship enough to get free of a sandbar and get the men to safety.

The captain was forced to surrender the ship to the local townspeople, reportedly handing his sword to one of the leaders from Truro, saying "Save the men and the ship will be yours."

The sailors of the *Somerset* eventually made it to land and safety. Several hundred men and women from Truro met them on shore.

The townspeople salvaged what they could from the *Somerset*. Some historians claim there are homes still standing in Truro today built using lumber from the ship.

Remarkably, 16 cannons from the *Somerset* were eventually delivered to Paul Revere in Boston to help protect the city from possible British attack.

The story of the HMS *Somerset* lives on today. Wooden beams from the ship still remain where the ship ran aground over 200 years ago. Several times since then, heavy storms and erosion have uncovered the remains of the ship, most recently in 2010. When visiting Cape Cod, you can go to the site where the *Somerset* still lays.

John Hancock's Trunk

We know a lot about the heavy wooden trunk that Paul Revere and John Hancock's clerk, John Lowell, hid from the British on the morning of April 19th, 1775. It contained a number of letters, correspondence, and information that would have been disastrous to the patriot cause if the British had gotten hold of it.

While things from history can often seem distant, you can still visit the wooden trunk that Paul Revere and John Lowell carried to safety. It's on permanent exhibit at the Worcester Historical Museum in Worcester, Massachusetts. The trunk is usually displayed during the month of April to celebrate the anniversary of the Battles of Lexington and Concord.

John Lowell and his newborn son, Francis

Following the events of April 1775, John Lowell went on to a distinguished legal career. He served as a delegate to the Continental Congress and later was appointed one of the United States' first federal judges by President George Washington.

John Lowell's newborn son, Francis Cabot Lowell, was just 12 days old at the time his father was carrying the heavy trunk through a crowd of militia on Lexington Green. Francis himself went on to greatness, helping establish the textile industry in New England. In fact, the town of Lowell, Massachusetts, was named after him.

Who Fired the First Shot?

On the Lexington Green on the morning of April 19, 1775, the first shots of the American Revolution were fired. Paul Revere, William Lowell, Captain John Parker, the 77 militia from Lexington, along with hundreds of British soldiers were all witnesses to that moment.

One of the great mysteries that remains is who fired the first shot that started the battle and the war. It's a mystery that will probably never be solved.

Eyewitnesses on both sides disagree on what they heard and saw. Many believed it sounded like a pistol shot. Paul Revere saw a puff of white smoke in front of the British soldiers.

Whether the shot came from a nervous British soldier somewhere in line or someone on the American side hidden nearby, we will never know.

John Hancock and Samuel Adams

John Hancock and Samuel Adams had illustrious careers following the events in April 1775.

John Hancock would go on to play a very important role in the American Revolution. Shortly after the battle, he traveled to Philadelphia to attend the Second Continental Congress, and he was named president of the Continental Congress from 1775 to 1777.

He is probably best known for his signing of the Declaration of Independence. He was first to sign his name to the historic document, using large, bold letters, reminding us of his confidence and his patriotism.

Even today, when being asked to sign a document, you may be asked to "put your John Hancock" on the page.

After America won the war and earned her independence, he was elected governor of Massachusetts until his death in 1793, at the age of fifty-six.

Following the Battles of Lexington and Concord, Samuel Adams continued to play a very important role in the American Revolution. After escaping from Lexington, he made his way to Philadelphia to attend the Second Continental Congress.

He was a strong supporter of independence from Britain, working with his cousin John Adams, Thomas Jefferson, Benjamin Franklin and others. He was one of the 56 signers of the Declaration of Independence in 1776.

Sons of Liberty

The Sons of Liberty was an important group of patriots dedicated to American independence. They always met in secret. Their activities would have been considered treason by the king, and if they were caught, they could be hanged as traitors.

Paul Revere, Dr. Joseph Warren, and a number of the most important patriot leaders of the time were members of the Sons of Liberty.

One of their most famous actions was the Boston Tea Party. Both Paul Revere and Joseph Warren participated, helping dump the English tea into the Boston Harbor as a show of defiance against King George III for the laws he had put in place.

As careful as they were to protect their identity, Revere, Warren and the others would have been shocked to learn that one of their own members, Dr. Benjamin Church, was actually a spy on behalf of General Gage!

Thanks to Church's reports, Gage knew many of their plans and the names of many of their members. He could have rounded them up and had them hanged for treason, but instead he decided to keep an eye on their actions through the spying of Dr. Church.

Even today, the Sons of Liberty are an important emblem of the fight for America's independence.

Dr. Warren's Informant

Prior to the British march on Lexington and Concord, Dr. Joseph Warren was able to obtain specific details about the British plans from a secret source. To find out such important information, his source must have been very close to the British leadership.

General Thomas Gage planned the attack on Concord and kept his plans extremely secret. Not even the soldiers who were part of the mission knew where they were headed until after they began to march toward Lexington and Concord.

General Gage kept his plans so secret that he had told only two people before the mission began. One was Lord Percy, a trustworthy British officer. By the time Lord Percy left his meeting with General Gage and was walking through the streets of Boston, he heard local townspeople talking about the secret plans. He was shocked.

He hurried back to General Gage to tell him that the plans had been disclosed, and Gage was crushed. He had only told one other person. His wife!

Margaret Kemble Gage, General Gage's wife, was an American and loved her country. She felt torn by having to support her husband, while still caring deeply for America. She hated the idea of her husband possibly being an instrument of war against her home country.

While there isn't concrete proof that she was Dr. Warren's source about the British plans that night, we do know that General Gage was so upset afterwards that he sent his wife to England while he remained in America. Their relationship was never the same.

So, while Dr. Warren never disclosed his secret source, many people then and now suspect it was General Gage's wife, Margaret.

Glossary

A

artillery – Large guns used in battle.

artisan – A skilled worker who makes things by hand, such as a blacksmith, silversmith or carpenter.

B

boiling point –When frustration, anger, or tension builds up between two groups and is about to explode, like water turning into steam.

British – People from England.

British regulars – The professional soldiers of Great Britain's army.

Buckman Tavern – A meeting place in Lexington, Massachusetts, where colonial militia gathered before the first battle of the American Revolution.

C

Cambridge, Massachusetts – A city near Boston that played an important role in the American Revolution.

cartridge boxes – Small containers used by soldiers to carry gunpowder and bullets.

Charlestown – A town near Boston that played a key role in the American Revolution.

Charlestown Neck – A narrow strip of land connecting Charlestown to the mainland.

clergyman – A religious leader, such as a minister or priest.

Coercive Acts – a set of laws established by King George III to punish the colonists for the Boston Tea Party. Known by the Americans as the Intolerable Acts.

column of soldiers – A long line of soldiers marching together.

commander in chief – The leader of an army or military force.

colonist – A person living in the American colonies under British rule before the United States became independent.

D

deacon – A church leader who helps with religious services and community work.

Declaration of Independence – A document written in 1776 that announced the American colonies were breaking away from Great Britain.

E

element of surprise – A military tactic where one side attacks suddenly to catch the enemy off guard.

erosion – The wearing away of land by wind, water, or other natural forces.

exhibit – A display of important objects, often in a museum.

eyewitnesses – People who see an event happen and can describe it.

F

ferry landing – A dock or area where boats carry people and goods across a river or body of water.

foot soldiers – Soldiers who fight on foot instead of on horseback or in vehicles.

fusilier – A soldier trained to use a musket, a common firearm in the 1700s.

G

Great Britain – A country made up of England, Scotland, Northern Ireland and Wales. The United States was originally a colony of Great Britain until America won its independence by winning the Revolutionary War.

H

harbor – A place along the coast where ships can dock safely.

I

illustrious – Famous or well-known for doing something great.

informant – A person who secretly gives information, often about an enemy's plans.

K

King George III – The King of Great Britain during the American Revolution. He supported laws and taxes that many American colonists believed were unfair, which led to a war for independence.

L

Lexington Green – A grassy area in Lexington, Massachusetts, where the first shots of the American Revolution were fired.

liberty – The right to be free and make one's own choices.

loyalists – People in the American colonies who remained loyal to Great Britain during the Revolution.

M

marshland – Low, wet land with many plants and moisture.

military offensive – A planned attack by an army.

military stores – Weapons and supplies for soldiers, such as muskets, gunpowder and cannons.

Minutemen – Colonial soldiers who were ready to fight at a moment's notice.

mission – A special task or job, often dangerous.

muskets – Long, old-fashioned guns used during the American Revolution, similar in shape to today's shotgun or rifle.

musket balls – Small, round lead bullets used in muskets, the main guns of the Revolutionary War.

N

naval blockade – A military strategy where warships prevent ships from entering or leaving enemy ports to cut off supplies and trade. At the start of the American Revolution, the British used naval blockades to cut off Boston from receiving supplies by sea. This was meant to punish the city for the Boston Tea Party and to force the colonists to obey British laws.

P

patriot – A person who supported American independence from Britain.

patriot cause – The movement by American colonists to gain independence from Britain.

patrol – A group of soldiers or guards watching an area for danger.

plot – A secret plan.

provisions – Supplies, like food and weapons, needed for a journey or battle.

R

raid – A sudden attack on an enemy.

reverend – A title for a Christian religious leader.

S

saddlehorse – A horse trained and used for riding rather than pulling carts or wagons.

sandbar – A strip of sand built up by waves, often found near shorelines.

sexton – A person who takes care of a church and its property, sometimes ringing the church bells.

silversmith – A person who makes things out of silver. Paul Revere was a skilled silversmith in Boston, known for creating fine silver items like teapots, spoons, and bowls. His craftsmanship was highly respected, and his shop became one of the most successful in the colonies.

Sons of Liberty – A group of colonists who protested against British rule. They used speeches, secret meetings, and bold actions—like the Boston Tea Party—to rally others to resist British rule.

steeple – A tall, pointed tower on a church.

T

treason – The crime of betraying one's country. The punishment was often death by hanging.

turning the tables – Changing a situation so that the person at a disadvantage gains the upper hand.

W

warship – A ship built for battle. At the start of the American Revolution, several British warships were stationed in Boston Harbor to enforce British laws and protect loyal officials. The British warships in Boston carried dozens of cannons. Their firepower would have been able to destroy enemy ships or bombard targets on land.

wharf – A platform where ships load and unload goods.

wine cask – A large wooden barrel used for storing wine.

Timeline of the American Revolution

Pre-War Tensions

1754–1763 – French and Indian War (also called the Seven Years' War) – Britain and the colonies fought against France and its Native American allies. After the war, Britain was heavily in debt, leading to new taxes on the colonies.

1764 – Sugar Act – Taxed sugar, molasses, and other goods

1765 – Stamp Act – Required stamps (a direct tax) on legal documents, newspapers, and playing cards. This was the first direct tax on the colonies, leading to the call for "No taxation without representation."

1765 – Quartering Act – Required colonists to provide housing and supplies to British troops stationed in America.

1766 – Stamp Act Repealed

1767 – Townshend Acts – Imposed duties on imported goods like glass, tea, paper, and paint. Sparked boycotts and protests led by groups like the Sons of Liberty.

1770 – Boston Massacre

1773 – Tea Act – Allowed the British East India Company to sell tea directly to the colonies at a lower price but kept the tax, undercutting colonial merchants.

1773 (December 16) – Boston Tea Party

1774 – Intolerable Acts (also called the Coercive Acts)

1774 – First Continental Congress meets.

The War Begins

1775 (April 18-19) – Paul Revere's Ride

1775 (April 19) – Battles of Lexington and Concord ("The Shot Heard 'Round the World")

1775 (May 10) – Second Continental Congress gathers in Philadelphia.

1775 (June 17) – Battle of Bunker Hill

1775 (July 3) – George Washington takes command of the Continental Army.

1775 (July 5) – Olive Branch Petition sent to King George III.

1775 (November-December) – Battle of Quebec (Failed American invasion of Canada.)

Declaration & Early Struggles

1776 (January) – Common Sense is published by Thomas Paine.

1776 (July 4) – Declaration of Independence adopted.

1776 (July 5) – The king rejects the Olive Branch Petition.

1776 (August 27) – Battle of Long Island (New York campaign, British victory)

1776 (September-October) – Battles of Harlem Heights & White Plains

1776 (December 26) – Battle of Trenton (Washington crosses the Delaware. American victory changes the course of the war.)

Turning the Tide

1777 (January 3) – Battle of Princeton (American victory that further boosts morale)

1777 (September 11) – Battle of Brandywine (British victory, capture of Philadelphia)

1777 (October 4) – Battle of Germantown (Failed American attack on British in Philadelphia)

1777 (October 17) – Battle of Saratoga (The American victory leads to an alliance with France.)

1777–1778 (Winter) – Valley Forge (Washington's army endures harsh winter. Baron von Steuben begins to train the soldiers.)

Allied Support & Southern Campaigns

1778 (February 6) – France officially joins the war on the American side.

1778 (June 28) – Battle of Monmouth (American tactical victory)

1779 (September 23) – Naval battle between John Paul Jones & HMS *Serapis* ("I have not yet begun to fight!")

1780 (May 12) – Siege of Charleston (British capture Charleston, SC)

1780 (August 16) – Battle of Camden (British victory, major American defeat)

1781 (January 17) – Battle of Cowpens (American victory in the South)

1781 (March 15) – Battle of Guilford Courthouse (Costly British victory)

Final Victory

1781 (October 19) – Battle of Yorktown (The British surrender, effectively ending the Revolutionary War.)

Independence

1783 (September 3) – Treaty of Paris signed (Britain recognizes America's independence)

Resources and acknowledgements

If you would like to learn more about Paul Revere and the American Revolution, there are many excellent resources about his famous ride on April 18th and 19th, 1775.

Here are a few examples:

1. *"Letter from Paul Revere to Jeremy Belknap, circa 1798."* Around 1798, Paul Revere wrote a letter to Jeremy Belknap, corresponding secretary of the Massachusetts Historical Society. In the letter, he explains in detail his activities of April 18-19, 1775. He describes how Dr. Joseph Warren urged him to ride to Lexington to warn John Hancock and Samuel Adams of British troop movements and a possible attempt to capture them. He outlines the plans to place signal lanterns in the steeple of the

Old North Church and how two friends rowed him across the Charles River where he borrowed a horse and began his ride, and more. The complete letter is transcribed and available at https://www.masshist.org or by searching "Letter from Paul Revere to Jeremy Belknap, circa 1798."

2. The Paul Revere House still stands today only a few blocks from the Old North Church. It is open to the public most days and is a wonderful resource on the life and times of Paul Revere. Standing on the doorstep of Revere's home gives you a sense of how close he lived to the key events of the day, including the Old North Church, which is just a few blocks away, the Long Wharf at Boston Harbor, and the many historic buildings in Boston's North End. The Paul Revere House offers tours, events and celebrations of one of the heroes of the American Revolution. For information about Paul Revere's home, visit https://www.paulreverehouse.org.

3. An outstanding book about Paul Revere is *Paul Revere's Ride* by David Hackett Fischer, © 1994, Oxford University Press. Mr. Fischer provides readers with a thorough, well-researched book. Those who love history are fortunate to have such an outstanding historical record of Paul Revere's life and times.

4. Dr. Joseph Warren, from whom the author is a direct descendent, played a vital role in the early efforts of the American Revolution. Historians note that he would certainly have played a key role in the formation of America had he not

been killed at the Battle of Bunker Hill just two months after Lexington and Concord. There are a number of letters and documents from Dr. Warren, but his address to the Massachusetts Provincial Congress on April 26th, 1775, gives readers an important account of the events just days afterwards. The transcript of the speech that he gave that night can be found at https://louis.pressbooks.pub by searching "Address from Joseph Warren."

5. The Paul Revere Heritage Project provides a wonderful source of information about Paul Revere, including his biography, his famous ride, and more. This site is another example of the excellent resources available for readers, teachers and parents looking to learn more about the hero of the "midnight ride," his life and his fellow patriots: http://www.paul-revere-heritage.com.

Test Your Understanding

1. What were some of the reasons the Americans wanted independence from Britain?

2. What is the difference between being ruled by a king vs. choosing your own government leaders?

3. If you had lived in America at the time, would you have been on the side of the loyalists who followed the king or on the side of those wanting independence? Why?

4. Why was King George III angry at the American colonists?

5. How do you think the loyalists felt when their neighbors began the fight for independence?

6. How do you think the patriots felt about the loyalists who would not join their cause?

7. If you were General Gage, what would you have done to stop the Sons of Liberty?

8. Minutemen had to be ready to go into battle on a moment's notice. What do you think are some items they would need to have ready before heading to battle? Where would they keep these items in the house?

9. Why would Dr. Benjamin Church spy on his fellow Sons of Liberty?

10. How would America be different today if the patriots had lost the Revolutionary War?

About the Author

W. Dean Kline is a historian and author specializing in nonfiction American history for both children and adults. His work explores pivotal eras, including the American Revolution, the Civil War, World War I, World War II, and America's journey into the Space Age.

In addition to his writing, Dean has over 30 years of experience in the technology sector, focusing on public relations and marketing.

Growing up in Wilton, Connecticut, Dean developed an early love of history with a special passion for the American Revolution. He holds a degree in English from Ohio Wesleyan University. Dean and his wife, Kristine, reside in Central Texas.